# The Quinoa Cookbook

# Ken Jones

**To Karen, Sarah and Nathan**

# The Complete Guide to Cooking Quinoa

## Simple and tasty recipes

Disclaimer: Please be aware that I am not a nutritionist or diet expert. I am merely someone who has taken control of their diet and health and done something about it. You must do this for yourself and take responsibility for your own health. The Quinoa recipes will help you include Quinoa into your diet.

## Introduction

### 1. Why write a book about Quinoa?

We came across Quinoa some time ago and thoroughly enjoy using it in our cooking.  We are always looking to find different ways to cook our own food without all the preservatives and enjoying varying tastes.

When we discovered Quinoa we were struck by the fact that it is very easy to prepare and is quite versatile.  In this day and age of fast food and busy lifestyles, we felt this was an ideal food to investigate.

We were amazed that it had been around for so long and that it had so many uses.

We were also stunned to discover all the benefits that it holds.

In the following chapters we will share what Quinoa is, what benefits it has for pregnant Mums, Diabetics, people with food allergies, or food intolerances (although we would always suggest that you check with your doctor if you are on a restrictive diet), Vegetarians, Vegans, people who are overweight, etc.

We will also share a range of recipes, cooking methods, etc.

So – read on and enjoy.

## 2. What is Quinoa?

Quinoa (pronounced "keen-wah") is a South American plant, an ancient super-food that has been re-discovered in recent years. It is a fantastic source of protein & slow re-leasing carbohydrate suitable for meat lovers and vegetarians alike. It is a versatile food that can be used in salads, stir-fries, soups, stews, casseroles, etc.

As far as we can establish, Quinoa originated in South America and was used by the Ancient Incas. It was regarded as a sacred food and valued for its amazing properties. The seed, also known as Quinoa, is sometimes called Mother Grain ("chesiya mama").

Quinoa is a lot like millet to look at but is flattened with a pointed oval shape. Although not a true cereal grain, it can be treated as a grain in cooking and is usually cooked like rice (although it can be sprouted too).

## 3. Properties of Quinoa

Quinoa is classed as a vegetable protein which is easy to digest. It is brilliant when used as an ingredient in weight loss diets as its slow releasing carbohydrates help to maintain blood sugar levels (ideal for diabetics too). It is known to be beneficial to both kidney and bladder complaints as it contains all the essential amino acids.

It is a complete protein but much easier to digest than most meat proteins making it an ideal addition to both vegan and vegetarian diets. It also offers more Iron than other grains and contains high levels of Potassium and Riboflavin, to say nothing of B vitamins, B6, Niacin and Thiamine. It is also a good source of Zinc, Copper and Manganese.

Quinoa is also gluten free which is a very valuable find in foods. In the present climate of health foods being gluten free helps people who are on restricted diets. It is also useful for migraine sufferers and a very good choice for pregnant mums as it is a natural product.

## 4. What is Quinoa like to eat?

With regard to its taste, it is light and delicate – an ideal substitute for almost any other grain.  As it cooks, the external germ, which forms a band around each grain, spirals out, forming a tiny point or "tail".  Although the grain itself is soft and creamy, the "tail" gives it a crunchy property which gives Quinoa its own unique texture which seems to complement the delicate Quinoa flavour of the seed.

Quinoa is often used as a meat substitute in vegetarian dishes and can even be eaten raw when sprouted for salads.  It is also wonderful as a thickener in soups.

# Chapter 1: How to cook Quinoa

### The 5 main ways to use Quinoa

### 1. Basic method of cooking Quinoa

Quinoa is usually prepared in it's seed or grain form and is best cooked as rice.   Just like rice it becomes fluffy and expands to twice its size.

For ease it is generally bought in boxed form.   This is partly processed Quinoa and is quicker to use.

When harvested, Quinoa is covered by an outer waxy coating called saponin. This needs to be removed otherwise it will have an unpleasant taste. (If you have bought Quinoa with its original coating then it is important to rinse it vigorously then soak it in water for several hours before rinsing it again.)

It is highly unlikely that you will come across quinoa with the full coating still on. Quinoa that you buy in supermarkets has usually been pre-washed.

It is still worth quickly rinsing Quinoa under a tap before use for a minute just to be sure.

### Important notes to help you get the best from our recipes.

1. We have only included recipes using the **grain kind of Quinoa** in the main book because it is the most widely available. We have used the light coloured Quinoa and red Quinoa. Black Quinoa is not yet available in England.

2. In many of the recipes you will see that the ingredient is called "**cooked and prepared Quinoa**" This is the section that shows you how to do that cooking and preparing. The resulting cooked Quinoa is then used in the recipe.

3. If the recipe simply states Quinoa with a quantity then you do not need to pre-cook for that particular dish.

**Cooked and Prepared Quinoa**

**Step 1**

Rinse the Quinoa in a fine sieve with cold water. Do this a second time to make sure the Saponin coating is completely removed (if you have bought unprocessed Quinoa then it is very important to follow the soaking procedure mentioned above).

**Step 2**

Measure out one cup of Quinoa to two cups of water into a saucepan.

**Step 3**

Bring the mixture to the boil, stirring gently to ensure it does not stick to the pan. Once it boils, turn the temperature down and let it simmer for ten to fifteen minutes. If you want it crunchy then ten minutes will be enough – if you want it soft and fluffy then leave it for longer.

All the water should be absorbed while the Quinoa is simmering and it will expand two to three times its original size.

Now remove the pan from the heat.

**Step 4**

Your Quinoa is now ready to serve as a substitute for rice with curry, or to include as a part of one of your regular meals, or maybe with other flavourings

It is also ready to include in the recipes in this book where the recipe says "Cooked and prepared Quinoa"

**2. Absorption method of cooking quinoa**

This is similar to the basic method but the Quinoa absorbs the liquid in the recipe and does not need cooking separately beforehand. A good example would be in Quinoa Pilaf where all the moisture is absorbed into the Quinoa. This is similar to cooking with rice.

### 3. Baking with Quinoa

We have tried replacing ingredients in baking with some success.

The main point to note is that Quinoa hold moisture so the liquid in the original recipe needs to be reduced. For example in the Cheesy Scones recipe I find that no extra liquid is needed to bind the dough when I use Quinoa.

Without Quinoa the original recipe needs milk or water to be able to roll out the dough.

### 4. Soups & Casseroles

Quinoa acts as a thickener in soups and casseroles. This can give a soup recipe a lot of "body". It can turn a snack into a meal. It can be used instead of Lentils and Pearl Barley in this way.

### 5. Salads

Quinoa Salads must be one of the healthiest meals around. You have all the goodness of Quinoa mixed in with fresh vegetables and your favourite dressings. It can make a meal out of a salad because Quinoa is so substantial. You can keep them in the refrigerator and use for easy packed lunches. If you have recipes for salads that are rice based or couscous based try using Quinoa instead.

The salad recipes in this book are just a few of the variations you can try. Experiment all you can and it will nearly always taste great.

# Chapter 2: Nutritional Information

### 1. Nutritional information about Quinoa

Quinoa is difficult to place in a food category as it is neither a grain nor a cereal. In fact it is probably best thought of as a seed.   It has a very distinctive flavour and is so full of nutrition that it is aptly called the true Mother Grain of the Andes.

As it is gluten free and full of dietary fibre, Quinoa is known to be a superb option for food allergy sufferers.   This is because common allergens include seeds from the grass family like wheat and corn, while Quinoa although having leaves in its plant form, is not part of the grass family.   This means that it does not cause the same reactions in those prone to allergies as is caused by wheat, corn or even barley, oats or rye, etc.   It is even regarded as a healing plant and was used in some instances to fight infections.

It also has an amazingly wide range of Amino Acids and considered to be a good source of manganese and copper.   It was often regarded as good for stamina and eaten daily.

Quinoa is high in protein and complex carbohydrates while being low in fat but plentiful in vitamins and minerals.   In fact it seems to be a very complete food and was used by mothers while pregnant as well as when nursing infants (it is thought to help improve the quality of milk mothers produce while feeding).   Indeed, Quinoa has plenty of Calcium, Fat, Iron, and Phosphorus while having a good range of Vitamin B.   It even has Zinc and Potassium too.   You will see below a brief summary of Quinoa nutrition facts.

Indeed it is because of its make-up that Quinoa is so versatile.   It can be used instead of rice, as a side dish, in its sprouted form as part of a salad, as an ingredient in casseroles, a thickener in soups, - the list seems endless.   Indeed, now that it has been re-discovered, it seems destined to be a valued and versatile accompaniment to any diet.   The range of healthy nutrients makes it a vital food ingredient to both vegetarians and meat lovers.

We hope that you will enjoy our recipes and will soon be including this wholesome food in your everyday cooking.

## 2. Quinoa Nutrition Chart

**Typical values per 100g of quinoa grain.**

- Energy 1498kJ/355kcal
- Protein 12.4g
- Carbohydrate 60.5g
- Of which sugars 36.7g
- Fat 7.0g
- Of which saturates 0.7g
- Of which mono-unsaturates 2.3g
  - Of which oleic acid (omega 9) 1.7g
- Of which polyunsaturates 3.9g
  - Of which linoleic acid (omega 6) 2.6g
  - Of which alpha linoleic acid (omega 3) 0.5g
- Fibre 7.8g
- Sodium 2.7g

**Minerals mg per 100g**

- Phosphorus 295 (52% RDA)
- Magnesium 176 (63% RDA)
- Iron 4.3 (18.6% RDA)

Zinc 2.2 (14% RDA)

# Chapter 3: The Health Benefits of Quinoa

**A Look At Some Of The Health Issues That Quinoa Can Help With.**

### 1. Health Benefits

The ancient seed of Quinoa is so versatile and such an important source of nutrients that it has been referred to as the "gold" of the Incas. It is known to increase stamina, a useful aid in days gone by when "warriors" needed every bit of advantage they could get when their "people" were under attack.

However, such is the structure of Quinoa, it has the benefit of being a natural and complete protein.  This means that it has all the Amino Acids like Acid Lysine which is very important for the repair and growth of body tissue.

As shown below, it is known to be beneficial to the body in a number of ways – nature's natural remedy.

The information below has come from a wide range of numerous sources that we have found over a period of time. It is intended to be a summary of these sources. You will, we are sure, gain great health benefits from including Quinoa in your diet - however we are not medical people. We simply enjoy Quinoa and have found these benefits as we have cooked and eaten Quinoa.

### 2. Migraines & Hypertension

Riboflavin and magnesium are the natural aids in Quinoa for bad headaches.  They are known to help relax the blood vessels, which reduces constriction and so eases tension. Basically they help the body to function better which in turn eases the stress the body experiences when circumstances make it over work.

While no one claims it makes headaches go away, it can help and is known to reduce the frequency of migraine attacks.

### 3. Childhood Asthma

Many allergies are connected with grass seeds but Quinoa is not a grass.

It is a plant but is not known to produce serious allergic reactions in people. Asthma is the result of breathing difficulties that are made worse by tension. It is known to have triggers and often there is a family history of asthma.  It is known to have gotten worse over the years and many experts point to our modern living conditions as making it more prevalent.

While not all asthma attacks are caused by allergies which may or may not be avoidable, it is known that Quinoa helps to reduce body stress and helps to keep the airways open. It is recommended that children with asthma eat a whole food diet.

Many of the nutrients that we need are in Quinoa such as Magnesium which naturally helps to reduce spasms in the bronchial tubes. We know that many asthma sufferers are short of Vitamin B, minerals like Magnesium, Zinc and Iron all of which can be found in Quinoa.

Why not check out some of the recipes and see which ones are easiest to include in your child's diet.

### 4. Gallstones

This is another surprising area where Quinoa is known to be useful. It may not get rid of gallstones but it can help hinder their development.

Indeed this is another case where a wholesome diet rich in fibre can aid in the digestion of foodstuffs. As it is a soluble fibre it speeds through the intestines and reduces the need of increased bile production. Too much bile production helps to develop gallstones so this is another natural remedy for our bodies.

### 5. Type 2 Diabetes

Quinoa is rich in Magnesium which is a mineral that is essential in the body's ability to deal with glucose and insulin. Yet again there is evidence that Quinoa, as part of a whole food diets aids in the digestion of foods.

It is also known to increase Insulin sensitivity while reducing triglycerides (blood fats which need to be kept low in diabetics).

### 6. Heart Disease

Quinoa is known to prevent the clogging of arteries and veins which in turn helps to relieve stresses on the heart. The fat in Quinoa is good fat in that is low in cholesterol and can help reduce blood pressure thanks to the presence of potassium and magnesium.

In other words it is a good source of protein without the drawbacks of too much saturated fat and cholesterol.

## 7. Pregnant Mums

Quinoa is known to be an endurance food which gives energy. It is also known to be a good source of Iron which pregnant mums are always advised to increase in their diet.

It is good for tissue repair and development of teeth and bones. Along with the other benefits of Quinoa, it is a useful source of goodness that forming babies will demand in plenty as they grow.

It is also good for Mums when they are feeding as it will improve the quality of milk for new-born infants.

## 8. Cancer

Fibre is known to help combat cancer and Quinoa is a good source of soluble and insoluble fibre. These attributes help in the fight against cancer of the colon. Fibre is known to help prevent cancer and can help with the natural waste products and aid constipation.

## 9. Cataracts

Quinoa is thought to help prevent cataracts and may aid those with the condition.

Studies have shown that people who absorb about 99 grams of protein were only half as likely to develop nuclear cataracts(light is difficult to pass through the centre of the eye) while those with the greater polyunsaturated fats about 17 grams a day were 30 percent likely not to develop problems with the outer lens (corticular cataracts).

## 10. Summary

Nowadays, we are looking more and more to natural foods.

We all know the benefits of fibre in our diet but until more recently we have forgotten about Quinoa. It is by studying the diets of different peoples around the world and noticing the presence or absence of different diseases and symptoms that we are coming to the realization that our daily intake of different foods can make a difference to our general health and quality of life.

It would appear that Quinoa is an essential food and much nicer to include in our everyday lives – indeed it may reduce the need for or reliance on medication (obviously no-one should change prescribed medication intake without the agreement of their doctor).

It is brilliant for vegans as it is a complete protein and many of its natural attributes like Magnesium, Copper, Riboflavin, etc., are quite hard to include in a strict vegan diet.

When eaten quinoa is very filling and can be useful when dieting to lose weight as it reduces the need for volume eating. It helps stop the craving for more food because you feel full.

It is also effective in blood sugar control which is essential in aiding type 2 diabetes. Indeed it seems to supply many of the body's essential foods and naturally aids the body to repair, keep relaxed, and use nutrients more fully.

Having discovered Quinoa, we hope you find its natural benefits a bonus and added extra that comes with the package – an ingredient that you will keep in your larder and use regularly.

# Chapter 4: Soups

### 1. Quinoa & Tomato Soup

**Ingredients**

- 1/2 cup (100gm) of Quinoa
- 8 Ripe Medium Tomatoes (They must be ripe for the best flavour)
- 1 Onion
- 1 Clove Garlic - chopped
- 1 Tsp Oregano or Parsley
- 1/2 Tsp Mixed Herbs
- 4 cups (½ litre) Water

**Method**

1. Place the tomatoes, onion, mixed herbs and garlic into a saucepan with the water.
2. Bring to the boil and then simmer for 5 minutes.
3. Add the Quinoa and bring back to the boil.
4. Simmer for 15-20 minutes.
5. Blend the mixture in a food processor and serve with a garnish of oregano.

## 2. Quinoa & Lentil Soup

### Ingredients

- 1/2 cup (100gm) Quinoa
- 1/2 cup (100gm)Red or Brown Lentils
- 1 Onion
- 2 Sticks Celery
- 2 Carrots
- 1/2 Sweet Potato (or half a Swede)
- 8 cups (1 litre) of Stock or Water
- 1 Tsp Coriander
- 4/5 drops Tabasco Sauce
- Pinch Cumin
- Pinch Salt
- 1 Tbsp Olive Oil

### Method

1. Rinse the Quinoa and lentils thoroughly
2. Chop the celery, onion, carrots and sweet potato
3. Cook the vegetables in the olive oil for a few minutes then add all the remaining ingredients
4. Bring the soup to the boil and simmer for 25 minutes. Serve
5. You can serve this soup straight from the pan or blend it in a food processor before serving.

### 3. Chicken & Quinoa Soup

**Ingredients**

- 1/2 Cup (100gm) Quinoa
- 1 Tbsp Olive Oil
- 1 Onion - chopped
- 1 Stick Celery - chopped
- 2 Carrots - chopped
- 1 Cup Peas (100gm fresh or frozen )
- 1 Medium Size Chicken Breast - cut into small strips
- 8 Cups (1 litre) Stock (or water with stock cube)
- 4/5 Drops Tabasco Sauce
- Pinch of Mixed Herbs
- Salt and Pepper to taste

**Method**

1. Cook the chicken pieces in the olive oil to seal.
2. Add all the vegetables and cook for a further 2 minutes
3. Add all the remaining ingredients and bring to the boil
4. Simmer for 25 minutes and serve.

## 4. Vegetable Soup

### Ingredients

- 1/2 Cup (100gm) Quinoa
- 8 Cups (1 litre) Water
- 1 Carrot - chopped
- 1 Stick Celery - chopped
- 1 Onion - chopped
- 2 Tomatoes - chopped
- 1 Cup (100gm) Frozen Peas
- 1 Tsp Parsley - chopped
- 1/4 Swede or Turnip - diced
- 1 Vegetable Stock Cube
- Salt and Pepper
- 1Tbsp Olive Oil

### Method

1. Sauté Quinoa, carrots, celery, onions, swede and peas in the olive oil for 3/4 minutes
2. Add the remaining ingredients and bring to a boil.
3. Simmer for 30 minutes.
4. Season to taste and garnish with parsley.

## 5. Parsnip Soup

### Ingredients

- 1/2 Cup (100gm) Quinoa
- 3 Medium Parsnips - chopped
- 1/2 Swede or Turnip - chopped
- 2 Carrots - chopped
- 1 Medium Potato or Sweet Potato - chopped
- 8 Cups (1 litre) Water
- 1 Vegetable Stock Cube
- ½ Tsp Cinnamon
- ½ Tsp Nutmeg
- Salt and Pepper to taste

### Method

1. Place all the ingredients into a large saucepan and bring to the boil
2. Simmer for 25 minutes
3. Add salt and pepper to taste
4. Blend the mixture in a food processor and serve immediately

### 6.  Quinoa, Leek and Potato Soup in a Slow Cooker

In this Quinoa recipe the Quinoa is the thickening agent. If it is cooked for a long time, the Quinoa will thicken soups and sauces quite well.

**The ingredients are:-**

- 2 Very Large Leeks
- 1 Onion
- 2 Large Potatoes
- 1 Cup Quinoa
- 2 Pints Vegetable Stock
- Salt and Pepper to taste
- Olive Oil

**Method of cooking**

- Warm up your slow cooker for 20 minutes on high setting
- Slice the leeks and potatoes.
- Chop the onion
- Fry these ingredients in a large wok for 2 minutes
- Add the stock and salt and pepper
- Bring the mix to the boil
- Add the Quinoa and bring back to the boil
- Transfer the soup to the slow cooker.
- Cook on low setting for 5 - 6 hours.
- Just before serving purify the soup for 20 seconds.
- Serve on its own or with croutons

# Chapter 5: Main Courses

**1. Cauliflower Cheese**

**Ingredients**

- 1 Cup Home-made Bread Crumbs
- 1 1/2 Cups (250gm) Grated Cheese. Cheddar, Leicester or Gloucester is best
- 4 Cups (1/2 litre) Milk
- 1 Cauliflower
- 1/2 Cup (100gm) Quinoa
- Pinch Nutmeg
- Salt and Pepper to taste
- A Knob of Butter or Margarine

**Method**

1. Trim and wash the cauliflower, cut into florets
2. Cook cauliflower in salted water until tender. drain the cauliflower and place in an oven proof dish
3. To make the sauce bring milk to the boil then add the breadcrumbs, butter Quinoa, nutmeg, salt and pepper and half the cheese. Mix well and simmer very gently for 5 minutes.
4. Pour the sauce over the cauliflower and sprinkle the remaining cheese on top.
5. Place in a medium oven for 15 minutes to finish cooking and brown

Adjust the amount of cheese to suit your preference.

## 2. Quinoa Tomato Sauce with Baked Potato

**Ingredients**

- Good Sized Potatoes - for baking in the oven or microwave oven.
- Knob of Butter
- 1/2 Cup (100gm) Quinoa
- 1 Tin of Chopped Tomatoes (or 6 very ripe fresh tomatoes)
- 1 Clove Garlic Chopped
- 4 Medium Mushrooms - sliced
- 1 Onion - chopped
- 4 Tbsp Olive Oil
- 1 Tbsp Chopped Parsley
- 1/2 Cup White Wine (Optional)
- 2 Cups (250ml) Vegetable Stock (or Water)
- Salt and Pepper to taste

**Method**

1. Bake the potatoes in the oven as normal usually about an hour.
2. To make the sauce first flash fry the garlic, onion and mushrooms until the onion goes clear
3. Add all the remaining ingredients cover and slowly simmer for 20 minutes, turning regularly. The sauce will thicken with the Quinoa.
4. Serve the potatoes with the knob of butter well worked into the potato before topping with the sauce.

### 3. Savoury Quinoa Pancakes

**Ingredients**

- For the batter
- 1 Cup (150gm) Flour
- 1/2 Cup (100gm) of Cooked and Prepared Quinoa
- 1 Large Egg
- 4 Cups (1/2 litre) Milk
- 1 Tbsp Olive Oil
- For the filling
- 1 Pepper Chopped
- 1/2 Tin Chopped Tomatoes
- 1 Small Onion
- 1 Garlic Clove
- 1/2 Courgette
- 1/2 Tspn Mixed Herbs

**Method**

1. For the pancake place the flour in a mixing bowl, add the egg, the olive oil and 1/2 of the milk. Beat to loose batter.
2. Add the rest of the milk and the prepared Quinoa to the mix.
3. Fry 2 tablespoons of the mix in an omelette pan until brown underneath. Turn and cook for a minute more.
4. Place pancake on plate and top with the sauce. Place a second pancake on top of the sauce for a pancake sandwich.
5. For the sauce flash fry the pepper, onion, garlic and courgette for 5 minutes.
6. Add the chopped tomatoes and herbs and simmer for 5 minutes

## 4. Quinoa & Potato Cake

### Ingredients

- 4 Medium Potatoes - grated
- 1 Onion - chopped
- 2 Tbsp Chopped Parsley
- 1/2 Cup (100gm) Cooked and Prepared Quinoa
- 1 Egg - beaten
- 2 Tbsp Olive Oil

### Method

1. Mix all the ingredients except the olive oil in a large bowl
2. Heat the oil in a frying pan and put all the mixture in to the pan to make a thick cake.
3. heat on low setting for 6/7 minutes
4. Turn the potato cake over and cook for a further 6/7 minutes until crispy and brown
5. Cut into wedges and serve immediately

## 5. Meatballs in Tomato Sauce

### Ingredients:

For the Meatballs

- 1 lb Lean Ground Beef
- 1/2 Cup (100gm) Cooked and Prepared Quinoa
- Approximately 1/3 Cup (100ml) Water (see instructions)
- 1/4 Cup Grated Parmesan Cheese
- 1 Medium Egg (optional but helps the meatballs bind together)
- 1 Medium Onion - chopped finely
- 2 Cloves Garlic - chopped
- Salt and Pepper to taste

For the sauce

- 1 Can Chopped Tomatoes
- 1 Clove Garlic - chopped
- 1 Onion - chopped
- 1 Tsp Fresh Basil

### Method:

1. Mix all the meatball ingredients together.
2. Only add the water if the mix is too dry to hold together.
3. Mixture should be moist but not so moist that the meatballs fall apart.
4. Make mixture into balls and place on a greased oven proof dish
5. Combine the sauce ingredients well and pour over the meatballs.
6. Cook in a medium oven for 30 minutes. Baste the meatballs every 10 minutes

## 6. Chilli Quinoa

**Ingredients**

- 1 Cup (200gm) Quinoa
- 1 Onion - chopped
- 1 Can Chopped Tomatoes
- 1 Can of Kidney Beans
- 1/2 Tsp Chilli Powder (depending how you like it)
- 1 Clove Garlic
- 1lb Minced Beef
- Salt and Pepper
- 4 Cups (1/2 litre) Stock or Water

**Method**

1. Fry onion and minced beef in a pan
2. Add chilli powder garlic and salt and pepper.
3. Add the stock, tomatoes and kidney beans and Quinoa
4. Simmer for 20 minutes
5. Serve on a bed of cooked and prepared Quinoa

**Vegetarian alternative** for Chilli Quinoa. Substitute Chick Peas and Root Vegetables for the Minced Beef.

## 7. Liver Mix

### Ingredients

- 1/2 Cup (100gm) Quinoa
- 1 Cup Flour - to coat the liver
- 1 lb Liver (Pork or Lamb)
- 2 Tbsp Olive Oil
- 2 Onions
- 2 Tomatoes - sliced
- 1 Cup Red Wine
- 2 Cups (1/4 litre) Stock or Water
- 2 Tbsp Tomato Puree
- 1 Tsp Mixed Herbs
- 1 Tbsp Parsley - chopped

### Method

1. Mix the flour, mixed herbs, salt and pepper with the flour and coat the liver with the mixture.
2. Heat the liver in the olive oil for 3/4 minutes. then put to one side.
3. Add the onions to the pan you cooked the liver in for 3 minutes.
4. Add the wine, stock, tomato puree, Quinoa and tomatoes to the mixture.
5. Bring to the boil and add the liver.
6. Simmer gently for 20 minutes and serve with a garnish of parsley.

## 8. Sausage & Mash

### Ingredients

- 1/2 Cup (100gm) Cooked and Prepared Quinoa
- 1 lb Potatoes
- 3 Spring Onions - finely chopped
- Knob of Butter
- Salt and Pepper
- Sausages of your choice

### Method

1. Fry the sausages in a frying pan.
2. Boil the potatoes until soft enough to mash. Drain.
3. Mash the potatoes with the knob of butter.
4. Add the Quinoa, spring onions, salt and pepper and mash once more.
5. serve with cooked sausages

## 9. Quinoa Burgers

### Ingredients

- 1 Cup (200gm) Cooked and Prepared Quinoa
- 4 Carrots
- 2 Sticks Celery
- Handful of Dark Green Cabbage Leaves
- 1 Large Onion
- 4 Eggs
- 2 Tbsp Olive Oil
- 1 Cup (150gm) Frozen Peas
- 1 Cup (150gm) Flour
- Salt and Pepper
- Herbs or Spices of your choice to flavour. (Try Mild Curry Flavour!)

### Method

1. Finely chop the carrots, celery, onion and cabbage in a food processor.
2. Add all the other ingredients and work into a rough dough.
3. Take handfuls of the mixture and shape into burgers.
4. Place on a greased baking tray
5. Cook in medium oven for 30 minutes.
6. These burgers can be frozen after cooking but must be defrosted fully before re-heating in the oven for 10 minutes.

## 10. Baked Courgette Pie

### Ingredients

- 1/2 Cup (100gm) Cooked and Prepared Quinoa
- 2 Tbsp Olive Oil
- 3 Large Courgettes - sliced
- 1/4 Cup Margarine
- 1/4 Cup Flour
- 2 Cups (1/4 litre) Milk
- 3 Eggs - separated
- Pinch Nutmeg

### Method

1. Fry the courgettes slowly in the olive oil for 10 minutes
2. Remove from the pan.
3. Melt the margarine in the pan and stir in the flour.
4. Add the milk and stir well
5. Bring mix to the boil slowly
6. Simmer for 3 minutes
7. Cool slightly then add the egg yolks, courgettes, salt and pepper and nutmeg to taste.
8. Whisk the egg whites until stiff and carefully fold into the mixture. Turn the mixture into a greased oven-proof dish.
9. Cook in a medium oven for 1 hour or until the pie has risen and set.

### 11. Cheese & Onion Flan

**Ingredients**

- 1/4 Cup (50gm) Quinoa
- 1 Cup Home-made Breadcrumbs
- 1 Cup (100gm) Grated Cheese
- 1 Onion - chopped
- 2 Eggs
- 2 Cups (1/4 litre) Milk
- Pinch of Paprika
- Salt and Pepper to taste
- Short Crust Pastry Base - part-baked.

**Method**

1. Beat the eggs and milk together.
2. Mix with the Quinoa, breadcrumbs, cheese, onion, salt and pepper.
3. Put mixture into the part baked pastry case and cook in a medium oven for 30 - 40 minutes until the flan sets

Serve with a mixed green salad

## 12. Quinoa with Herbs and Nuts

This recipe was taken from a packet of <u>Granovita</u> Quinoa. This Quinoa recipe demonstrates one of the 4 cooking methods for Quinoa very well because you do not need to pre-cook the Quinoa.

### Ingredients

1 1/2 Cups Granovita Organic Fairtrade Quinoa
1 Cup Cashew Nuts
2 Courgettes
Bunch of Spring Onions
Thyme
Parsley
Olive Oil
Sea Salt

### Method

1. Wash the onions and chop the green part into small pieces.
2. Scrub the courgettes, remove the ends and chop into small chunks.
3. Grill the nuts for a few minutes in a dry pan.
4. Fry the courgettes and the green of the onions in the oil, stirring continuously
5. When the vegetables are well cooked, add the Quinoa, the cashew nuts    and a teaspoon of thyme.
6. Add salt and mix until the Quinoa has absorbed all the moisture.
7. Place the white of the onions (whole) in the frying pan and pour in 3 g   lasses of water. Do not stir.
8. Leave to simmer for 20 minutes over a gentle heat.
9. Garnish with fresh parsley and serve hot.

### 13. Quinoa Pilaf Recipe

This simple quinoa pilaf recipe is taken from a Granovita packet. You can adapt it by changing the fruit or juice flavour. You can also blend chopped fresh fruit with it just before serving and put a dollop of cream on top.

Serves 8 -10
Preparation and cooking time - 30 minutes


Ingredients

1 Cup Quinoa
3 Cups Orange Juice
1/2 Cup Raisins (currant or dried cranberries)
1 Tbsp Lemon Zest
1 Tbsp Olive Oil


Method

Heat olive oil, add lemon zest and quinoa.

Sauté until Quinoa starts to heat and the aroma of lemons is strong.

Add dried fruit, stirring to coat.

Add orange juice and steep until all liquid is absorbed.

Great as a meal accompaniment or as a breakfast dish.

## 14. Quinoa Tabouleh

This recipe is taken from a packet of Quinoa from <u>Infinity Foods</u>.
This is really a type of Quinoa Salad and is a good method of preparing the Quinoa dish ahead of the serving time and keeping it in the fridge.

**Quinoa Tabouleh**

**Ingredients**

- 250g Cooked and Cooled Quinoa
- 3 Chopped Tomatoes
- 4 Chopped Spring Onions
- 1 Small Cucumber - finely diced
- 2 Large Garlic Cloves - minced
- 2 Tablespoons of Olive Oil
- 2 Tablespoons of Lemon Juice
- Handful of Pine Kernels (optional)
- Bunch of Freshly Chopped Mint
- Bunch of Freshly Chopped Parsley
- Salt & Pepper

**Method**

Combine the first 8 ingredients and chill for an hour
Prior to serving mix in the freshly chopped mint and parsley
Season to taste with salt and pepper

# Chapter 6: Salads

## 1. Simple Quinoa Salad

### Ingredients

- 1/2 cup (100gm) of Quinoa Grain Cooked and Prepared
- 1 Stick of Celery
- 1 Carrot
- 1/2 an Onion (Or 3 medium Spring onions)
- 1 Green Pepper (Or any colour you like)
- Salad Leaves
- Italian Balsamic Syrup (Or your preferred Dressing)

### Method

1. Chop the celery, onion and pepper.
2. Slice the carrot thinly (I use a potato peeler to give me carrot shavings)
3. Toss the ingredients together with the prepared quinoa.
4. Place on a bed of salad leaves and drizzle with the Italian Balsamic Syrup

Can be eaten solo or with cold meat, boiled eggs or fish

The Quinoa in this salad can be cooled for this dish in a refrigerator

Alternatively you can serve it immediately added from the hot pan for a "warm Salad"

**Simple Salad Variations.** Substitute the carrot, celery and the green pepper with the following ingredients.

A. Waldorf salad. Celery, Apple, Walnuts and Rocket.
B. Salad with a bite. Water cress, spinach, radishes and beetroot.
C. Oriental salad. Bean sprouts, noodles and rocket.
D. Completely green Salad. Any salad leaf, cucumber, celery and Chives
E. Very red salad. Red pepper, tomato, radishes and red cabbage.

### Wrap it up in a tortilla wrap.

All of the above salads can be put in a tortilla wrap with cold meat. This is an ideal packed lunch idea.

## 2. Mixed Bean Salad

### Ingredients

- 1/2 Cup (100gm) Cooked and Prepared Quinoa
- 1 Can of Mixed Haricot and Kidney Beans. (I actually use dried beans and do the whole soak and boil routine but then I am a bit of a food fanatic.)
- 1 Green Pepper - chopped
- 1 Tbsp Pine Nuts
- Fresh Salad Leaves
- 1/2 Cup French Salad Dressing (Or your own favourite dressing)

### Method

1. Rinse the beans
2. Mix with the chopped pepper, pine nuts and quinoa
3. Toss in the salad dressing
4. Serve on the fresh salad leaves

**Bean Salad Variations.** Substitute the haricot/kidney beans, pine nuts and green pepper with the following ingredients.

A. Chick pea salad. Chick peas. Walnuts and celery
B. Fresh bean salad. Broad beans, peas and tomatoes

### 3. Tangy Salad

**Ingredients**

- 1/2 Cup (100gm) of Cooked and Prepared Quinoa - COOLED
- 1 Cup (100ml) Water
- 3/4 Spring Onions
- 1 Red Pepper
- 1/4 Cucumber - sliced
- 1/2 Cup (200ml) Orange Juice
- 1 Tsp Lime Juice
- 1 Tbsp Balsamic Syrup
- Pinch of Salt

**Method**

1. Prepare the vegetables and combine well with the cooled Quinoa.
2. Mix juices, syrup and salt together.
3. Combine the juice mixture with the Quinoa mix and serve

**4. Nutty Salad -** Probably the easiest recipe of all

**Ingredients**

- 1/2 cup (100gm) Cooked and Prepared Quinoa - cooled
- 3 Spring Onions - chopped
- 1 Red Pepper - chopped
- 1/2 Cup Raisins
- 1/2 Cup Roasted Cashew Nuts - chopped
- 2 Tbsp Chopped Parsley
- 6 Tbsp Soy Sauce

**Method**

1. Prepare all the ingredients
2. Mix well in a large bowl ensuring the soy sauce covers everything
3. Serve

### 5. Celery & Apple Salad

**Ingredients**

- 1/2 Cup (100gm) Cooked and Prepared Quinoa - cooled
- 4 Sticks Celery - sliced
- 3 Fresh Eating Apples - sliced
- 4 Tbsp French Dressing
- 1 Tbsp Roasted Sesame Seeds

**Method**

1. Place the Quinoa, apple and celery in a large bowl and mix well
2. Pour on the French dressing and toss well
3. Just before serving sprinkle the sesame seeds over the salad

## 6. Leaf & Warm Mushroom Salad

**Ingredients**

- 1/2 Cup (100gm) Cooked and Prepared Quinoa
- Hand Full of Cress Leaf
- Hand Full of Baby Spinach
- Hand Full of Rocket Salad
- 3 Spring Onions - chopped
- 6 Mushrooms - sliced
- 1 Tbsp Olive Oil
- 4 Tbsp French Dressing (Or dressing of your choice)

**Method**

1. Fry the mushrooms in the olive oil until soft and tender.
2. Toss the mushrooms with the other ingredients
3. Drizzle with French dressing and serve immediately

### 7. Potato& Beetroot Salad

**Ingredients**

- 1 lb Baby New Potatoes
- 1/2 Cup (100gm) Cooked and Prepared Quinoa
- 1 Large Cooked Beetroot - diced
- 1/4 Cucumber - diced
- 1 Cup (100ml) Natural Low Fat Yoghurt
- 1 Tbsp Dill - chopped
- 2 Tbsp French Dressing

**Method**

1. Cook the potatoes in their skins until they are soft and tender.
2. Drain and mix with the French dressing. Leave to cool.
3. Add the Quinoa, beetroot, cucumber and yoghurt dressing.

Mix well. Serve with a sprinkling of dill on top.

# Chapter 7: Snacks

## 1. Quinoa Flapjack "QUINJACK"

**Ingredients**

- 1/2 Cup (100gm) of Cooked and Prepared Quinoa
- 2 Cups (200gm) of Plain Flour
- 1 Cup 100gm) of Brown Sugar
- 1/2 Cup (50gm) Margarine or Butter
- 1/2 Cup (100gm) Golden Syrup
- Pinch of Cinnamon Powder

**Method**

1. Rub the Margarine/Butter into the flour until it is like breadcrumbs.
2. Add the remaining ingredients and mix well
3. Put mixture into greased baking trays and press the mixture into the trays so that it is about 10mm thick (1/2")
4. Cook in an oven for 20 minutes at a medium temperature until it starts to turn brown
5. Take out of the oven and cut into slices while in the trays.
6. Cool for 5 minutes and then finish cooling on cooling rack.

Store in the refrigerator in an air tight container

## 2. Cheesy Quinoa Scones

### Ingredients

- 1/2 Cup (100gm) Cooked and Prepared Quinoa
- 2 Cups (200gm) Self Raising Flour (you can also use plain flour and increase the amount of Baking powder and Bicarbonate of soda)
- 1/2 Tsp Baking Powder
- 1/2 Tsp Bicarbonate of Soda
- 1/2 Cup Margarine/Butter
- 1 Cup (150gm) Matured Cheddar Cheese - finely grated

### Method

1. Sieve the flour, baking powder and bicarbonate of soda into a mixing bowl
2. Rub in the margarine until the mix looks like small crumbs
3. Add the grated cheese and mix thoroughly
4. Add the Quinoa and make into a dough. (Add water or milk if the mix is a bit dry)
5. Roll out the dough and use a cookie cutter to cut the scones
6. Place on a greased cooking tray and cook in a hot oven for 12 minutes, or until the top starts to turn brown

### 3. Quinoa Dip

**Ingredients**

- 1 Ripe Avocado Pear
- 1/2 Cup (100gm) Cooked and Prepared Quinoa
- Juice of Half a Lemon
- 3 Spring Onions - chopped finely
- 2 Tomatoes - skinned and chopped
- 1/2 Tsp Worcestershire Sauce
- 1 Small Tub Natural Low Fat Yoghurt
- Salt and Pepper
- Carrots, Cucumber, Peppers and anything else you want to dip

**Method**

1. Get all the avocado out of the skin and mix with the Quinoa and lemon juice
2. Add the tomatoes, spring onions, Worcestershire sauce, yoghurt and salt and pepper to taste
3. Mix very well and turn out into a serving bowl.
4. Serve with vegetables of your choice for dipping

**4. Quinoa Hummous**

**Ingredients**

- 1/2 Cup (100gm) Cooked and Prepared Quinoa
- 1 Cup (200gm) Chick Peas, - soaked overnight (You can also use tinned chick peas)
- Salt and Pepper
- 2 Tbsp Olive Oil
- Juice of 1/2 Lemon
- 2 Tbsp Tahini (Sesame seed Paste)
- 2 Cloves Garlic

**Method**

1. Bring chick peas to boil and simmer until soft (about an hour)
2. Drain the chick peas keeping the water to add to the mix.
3. Put all the ingredients into a food processor with a good pinch of salt and pepper
4. While blending the mix add enough residue water to make the Hummous soft and creamy
5. Serve as a dip or on salad leaves with tomato and cucumber

## 5. Spinach Omelette

### Ingredients

- 1/2 Cup (100gm) Cooked and Prepared Quinoa
- 1/2 Cup (100gm)Margarine
- Handful of Fresh Spinach
- 1 Tbsp Natural Yoghurt
- 1 Cup (150gm) Grated Cheese
- Salt and Pepper
- 4 Eggs

### Method

1. Melt 1/2 the margarine in a pan and cook the spinach gently for 5 minutes.
2. Add the Quinoa salt and pepper and yoghurt and mix well.
3. Remove from heat and keep to one side.
4. Mix the eggs with salt and pepper in a bowl
5. Heat the remaining margarine in an omelette pan and pour in the eggs.
6. As the omelette begins to set, lift one side of the omelette up to pour any remaining egg mixture on to the pan.
7. When the egg is almost cooked put the spinach and Quinoa mix into the centre of the omelette.
8. Cook for a further minute then fold over in half
9. Sprinkle grated cheese over the top and serve.

## 6. Ginger Cake

### Ingredients

- 2 Cups (200gm) Self Raising Flour
- 1/4 Cup (50gm) Cooked and Prepared Quinoa
- 1 Cup (100gm) Sugar
- 1 Cup (200gm) Margarine
- 1 Apple - finely chopped
- 2 Tbsp Fresh Grated Ginger
- 2 Tsp Ground Ginger
- 1 Tsp Baking Powder
- 1 1/2 Cups (300ml) Milk
- 2 Eggs - beaten.

### Method

1. Cream together the butter and sugar
2. Add the beaten eggs and the milk. Beat well together
3. Add the Quinoa, flour and baking powder slowly
4. When the ingredients are combined add the apple and ginger.
5. Pour the mix into a cake tin lined with grease proof paper.
6. Bake in a medium oven for 1 hour or until the cake is firm.
7. Turn out cake and cool.

# Chapter 8: Stir Fry Dishes

### 1. Stir Fry Vegetables

**Ingredients**

- 1/2 Cup (100gm) Cooked and Prepared Quinoa
- 4 Tbsp Olive Oil
- 1 Onion
- 2 Carrots - cut into thin strips
- 1 Stick Celery
- 1 Green Pepper - sliced
- 4 Medium Mushrooms  - sliced
- 2 cups Bean Sprouts
- 1 Clove Garlic
- 1 Tsp Chopped Root Ginger
- 2 Tbsp Sherry (Optional)
- 2 Tbsp Soy Sauce
- Salt and Pepper

**Method**

1. Heat the olive oil in a wok or large pan.
2. Fry the garlic, onion, carrots, celery and pepper for 5 minutes. Turn constantly.
3. Add the prepared Quinoa mushrooms and bean sprouts and stir fry for a further 2 minutes
4. Add the sherry, soy sauce and salt and pepper. Stir fry for 3 minutes
5. Serve immediately

## 2. Ratatouille

**Ingredients**

- 1/2 Cup (100gm) Cooked and Prepared Quinoa
- 2 Tbsp Olive Oil
- 1 Red Pepper - chopped
- 1 Green Pepper - chopped
- 1 Onion - chopped
- 2 Stick Celery - chopped
- 1 Medium Courgette
- 1 Tbsp Tomato Puree
- 1 Can Chopped Tomatoes
- 4 Drops Tabasco Sauce (optional)
- 1 Tsp Fresh Basil

**Method**

1. Fry the peppers, onion, celery and courgette for 5 minutes in the olive oil.
2. Add the flavourings and the puree.
3. Finally combine with the chopped tomatoes and bring to the boil
4. Simmer gently for 5 minutes and serve.

### 3. Cajun Stir Fry

**Ingredients**

- 1/2 Cup (100gm) Cooked and Prepared Quinoa
- 2 Tbsp Olive Oil
- 1 Courgette - sliced
- 6 Mushrooms - sliced
- 1 Onion - chopped
- 1 Red Pepper
- 1 Tin Sweetcorn
- 1 Tsp Cajun Spice Mix (Or more to your taste)
- Salt and Pepper
- 5 Drops Tabasco Sauce

**Method**

1. Heat the oil in a large pan or wok
2. Fry the vegetables and Quinoa briskly for 5 minutes.
3. Add the spices and Tabasco sauce. Fry for 2 more minutes.
4. Serve with pitta bread, in a tortilla wrap or to accompany a main meal.

**4. Nutty Stir Fry**

**Ingredients**

- 1/2 Cup (100gm) Cooked and Prepared Quinoa - This time cooked for only 7/8 minutes so it is a bit crunchier.
- 1/4 Cup (50gm) Pine Nuts
- 1/4 Cup (50gm) Sunflower Seeds
- 1/4 Cup (50gm) Cashew Nuts - chopped
- 1 Carrot - cubed
- 1 Tbsp Sesame Seeds
- 1 Tbsp Olive Oil

**Method**

1. Heat the olive oil and flash fry the Quinoa and carrots for 3 minutes
2. Throw in the remaining ingredients and continue to cook fast for 2 minutes.
3. Serve.
4. You can store this in an air tight container in the refrigerator and have as a snack or quick lunch when you know you will be rushed.

## 5. English Stir Fry

### Ingredients

- 1/2 Cup (100gm) Cooked and Prepared Quinoa
- 1 Tbsp Olive Oil
- 1 Carrot - grated
- 1 Onion - chopped
- 1 Potato - grated
- Handful of Runner Beans - sliced. (Can use French beans but then that wouldn't be an English stir fry)
- Salad Leaves
- Cress
- Mixed Herbs
- 1/2 Tsp Parsley - chopped
- 1/4 Tsp Marjoram - chopped
- Salad Cream to dress (Or Mayonnaise)

### Method

1. Boil the runner beans briskly for 5 minutes. Drain and set aside.
2. Heat the oil in a large pan and fry the onion for 1 minute.
3. Add the potatoes and carrots and fry for 3 more minutes. Add the runner beans, Quinoa, and the herbs and fry for 2 minutes.
4. Serve with the cress and salads leaves and garnish with a dollop of salad cream.

# Chapter 9:  Desserts

### 1. Sweet Quinoa Pilaf

**Ingredients**

- 1/2 Cup (100gm) Quinoa
- 1 1/2 Cups (300ml) of Orange Juice
- 1/4 Cup of Raisins
- 1 Tbsp Lemon Zest
- 1 Tbsp Olive Oil
- Pinch of Nutmeg
- 2 Fresh Mint Leaves (optional)

**Method**

1. Heat the olive oil in a saucepan
2. Add the Quinoa, lemon zest and raisins and cook them for 1 minute
3. Add the orange juice, nutmeg and mint leaves.
4. Bring to slow boil and simmer until all the liquid is absorbed
5. Remove mint leaves and serve

This can be a dessert or breakfast dish. You can also use a different flavour fruit juice.

## 2. Quinoa Milk Pudding

**Ingredients**

- 1/2 Cup (100gm) Quinoa
- 1/2 Cup (100gm) Brown Sugar
- Pinch of Cinnamon
- 2 Eggs
- 1 1/2 Cup (300ml) Soya Milk (or goats milk)
- Fresh Fruit to top. Kiwi, apple, banana, strawberries - whatever you prefer.

**Method**

1. Place all the ingredients into a greased oven proof dish
2. Cook in the oven for 40 minutes in a medium heat or until the mixture is just set.
3. Stand for a further 10 minutes and serve with a topping of fresh fruit of your choice

### 3. Quinoa Fruity Porridge

**Ingredients**

- 1/2 Cup (100gm) Quinoa
- 1 Cup (200ml) Water
- 1 Apple - sliced
- 1/4 Cup Raisins or Currants
- Pinch of Cinnamon
- 1Tbsp Honey or Strawberry Jam

**Method**

1. Cook the Quinoa in the water for 10 minutes.
2. Add the apples, raisins and cinnamon.
3. Simmer until all the liquid is absorbed
4. Serve with a dash of honey or jam in the middle.

## 4. Fruity Salad

**Ingredients**

- 1/4 Cup (50gm) Cooked and Prepared Quinoa
- 1/3 Cup Mint - chopped
- 1/2 cup (100ml) Vanilla Flavoured French Set Yoghurt
- 2 Tbsp Orange Juice
- 1 cup Strawberries - sliced
- 1 Medium Kiwi Fruit - peeled and sliced
- 1 Cup Seedless Grapes

**Method**

1. Blend the yoghurt, mint and orange juice in a food processor
2. Combine the fruits and Quinoa in a bowl and then add the yoghurt mix.
3. Make sure all the fruit is covered in the yoghurt mix and chill in the refrigerator for 2 hours.
4. Garnish with a few kiwi and strawberry slices and serve

## 5. Fruit & Nut Mix

### Ingredients

- 1 Cup (200ml) Water
- 1 Cup (200ml) Apple Juice (or a whole apple juiced)
- 1/2 Tsp Cinnamon
- 1 Cup (200gm) Quinoa, - well rinsed and drained
- 2 Large Red Apples, - diced
- 1 Cup Chopped Celery
- 1/2 Cup Blueberries
- 1/2 Cup Chopped Walnuts
- 1 Cup (200ml) Non-fat Vanilla Yoghurt

### Method

1. Place water, apple juice, cinnamon and rinsed Quinoa in a saucepan
2. Bring to a boil.
3. Reduce heat, cover and simmer until all of the liquid is absorbed
4. Cool
5. Transfer Quinoa to a large mixing bowl and chill for 2 hours
6. Add apples, celery, blueberries and walnuts to Quinoa.
7. Mix well.
8. Fold in yoghurt.
9. Serve immediately.

## 6. Strawberry Crunch

### Ingredients

- 1/4 cup (50gm) Margarine
- 1 Cup Home-made breadcrumbs
- 1/4 Cup (50gm) Cooked and Prepared Quinoa
- 1/2 Cup (100gm) Soft Brown Sugar
- 1/4 Cup (50gm) Chopped Walnuts
- 1 Tub Natural Low Fat Yoghurt.
- 4 cups Fresh Strawberries - sliced

### Method

1. Melt the margarine in a frying pan
2. Add the breadcrumbs and Quinoa and cook until golden
3. Remove from the heat and add the walnuts and sugar.
4. Divide the mix into small dishes with the strawberries in alternate layers finishing with the mix.

Top each dish with a spoon of yoghurt and half a strawberry

### 7. Red Quinoa & Fruit Salad

Serves 1 - Preparation & Cooking time - 30 minutes

- 110g Red Quinoa,
- 300ml Water,
- 25g Raisins,
- 25g Pine Nuts,
- 25g Pineapple (Fresh or tinned),
- 1 Tbsp chopped Mint Leaves,
- 1 Spring Onion,
- 1 Tbsp Olive Oil,
- Pinch of Salt & Pepper

Rinse Quinoa well before cooking, Add Quinoa to 300ml of boiling water, return to boil and then reduce heat and simmer for approximately 10 minutes until germ separates. Remove from heat, cover and leave to absorb remaining water. Once the water has been absorbed leave to cool.

Combine remaining ingredients and mix well. Add Quinoa once cooled and mix gently. Serve immediately or refrigerate.

Can be served as a meal accompaniment or on its own as a snack

# Section Two - Cooking with Quinoa Flour and Flakes

### 1. Quinoa Flour and Flakes

The recipes here are a few early try outs of recipes. The bread ones work in our bread machine but as machines vary you may need to adapt them for your machine.

We have found that the texture is quite different from wheat flour and the recipes do not adapt easily without the inclusion of some wheat flour.

The problem with this is that if you are eating a wheat free diet then you cannot use these recipes. We have included a gluten free tortilla recipe.

### Bread Ideas

### Simple Quinoa Bread

### Ingredients

- 1 1/2 Cups Warm Water (can use milk)
- 2 Tbsp Olive Oil
- 1 Tsp Salt
- 2 1/2 Cups whole-wheat Flour
- 1 Cup Quinoa Flour
- 1 Tsp Dried Yeast

### Method

1. This recipe uses a bread machine.
2. Put the salt and water in the tin first
3. Cover with the flour and Quinoa flour
4. Top with the yeast
5. Cook on the basic programme (Kneads the dough twice)

**Bread Rolls**

Note: This recipe can be kneaded and prepared in the traditional way if preferred. I let the bread machine do all the hard work for me.

**Ingredients**

- 1 1/2 Cups Warm Water
- 1 Tsp Salt
- 1 Tsp Dried Yeast
- 1 1/2 Cups White Bread Flour
- 1 Cup Quinoa Flour
- 1 1/2 Cups Wholemeal Flour
- 2 Tbsp Margarine

**Method**

1. Put the warm water and salt into your bread maker
2. Mix the flours together and put on top of the water.
3. Put the dried yeast and margarine on top of the flour
4. Run the bread maker for the 2 kneading cycles then remove the dough from the bread maker
5. Break the dough into small balls place on a baking tray and allow to rise for 60 minutes in a warm place.
6. Put the risen rolls into a hot oven with a bowl of water in the bottom of the oven.
7. Cook for 20 minutes on hot then reduce the temperature to medium for a further 10 - 20 minutes of cooking.
8. Remove from the oven and cool.

**Fruit Bread** - Make as a loaf or into tea cakes.

**Ingredients**

- 1 1/2 Cups Warm Water (can use milk)
- 2 Tbsp Olive Oil
- 1 Tsp Salt
- 1/2 Cup Dried Fruit
- 2 Tbsp Clear Honey
- 2 1/2 Cups Whole-wheat Flour
- 1 1/2 Cups Quinoa Flour
- 1 Tsp Dried Yeast

**Method**

1. This recipe uses a bread machine.
2. Put the salt and water in the tin first
3. Cover with the flour and Quinoa flour
4. Top with the yeast, honey and dried fruit
5. Cook on the basic programme (Kneads the dough twice)
6. For tea cakes remove the mix after the second kneading and rise the teacakes in a warm draught free area for 1 hour. Cook in a hot oven for 12-15 minutes.

# Baking with Quinoa Flour

### Quinoa Cookies

### Ingredients

- 1/2 Cup Honey
- 1/2 Cup Crunchy Peanut Butter
- 1/2 Cup Soft Brown Sugar
- 1/2 Cup Butter or Margarine
- 1/2 Tsp Mixed Spice
- 1 Cup Quinoa Flour
- 1 Cup Quinoa Flakes
- 1/2 Tsp Salt
- 1 Tsp Baking Powder

### Method

1. Mix the honey, peanut butter, brown sugar and mixed spice to together.
2. Add the Quinoa flour, Quinoa flakes salt and baking powder
3. Mix thoroughly.
4. Put small mounds of mixture on a well greased cooking tin
5. Bake in a medium oven for about 12 minutes (until firm to touch)

**Quinoa Cake**

**Ingredients**

- 2 Cups Quinoa Flour
- 1 Cup Raisins or Currants
- 1/2 Cup Walnuts
- 1 Tsp Baking Powder
- 1/2 Tsp Salt
- 2/3 Cup Margarine or Butter
- 1 Cup Soft Brown Sugar
- 1 Large Egg
- 2 Apples Freshly Juiced

**Method**

1. Toss the walnuts and raisins in a small amount of the flour. Put aside.
2. Mix the remaining Quinoa flour with the salt and baking powder.
3. In a third bowl mix the apple juice, margarine, brown sugar and egg.
4. Add in the flour mixture and finally the fruit and nut mixture
5. Put the mixture into a greased cake tin and bake on a moderate oven for about 40 minutes

## Welsh Cakes

Note: This recipe is based on our favourite welsh cake recipe but with all the wheat flour replaced with Quinoa flour. Because of this the cakes have to be baked in the oven instead of on a griddle which is the traditional way. This is because the mixture doesn't bind as well as a wheat based mixture and won't hold together on the griddle.

### Ingredients

- 2 Cups Quinoa Flour
- 1 Tsp Baking Powder
- 1/2 Cup Margarine or Butter
- 1/2 Cup Caster Sugar
- Pinch of Salt
- 1/2 Cup Currants(optional)
- 1/2 Tsp Mixed Spice
- 1 Egg

### Method

1. Mix the flour, salt, mixed spice and baking powder together
2. Work in the margarine so that the mix looks like breadcrumbs
3. Add the sugar and currants
4. Add the egg add work the mixture into a dough. If it is too stiff add a little milk.
5. Put flat discs of the mixture on a greased baking sheet.
6. Cook for 12/15 minutes
7. Cool in the tin for 5 minutes before turning out onto a cooling tray.

**Oat Pancakes**

**Ingredients**

- 1 Cup Quinoa Flour
- 1 Cup Oat Bran
- Large Pinch of Salt
- 2 Tbsp Sugar
- 1 Tbsp Clear Honey
- 2 Eggs
- 3 Tbsp Olive Oil
- 1 Cup Milk
- 1 Cup Squeezed Orange Juice
- Zest of One Orange

**Method**

1. Mix the flour, oat bran, salt and sugar in a mixing bowl
2. In another bowl mix the honey, eggs, oil, milk, juice and zest.
3. Combine the 2 mixtures making sure not to over mix - you are looking for a thick batter.
4. Pour a portion of the batter into a frying pan to make the first pancake
5. Turn when the bottom is light brown
6. Cook the second side and serve with fruit or syrup.

### Quinoa Fruit and Nut bar.

This is a great snack bar to have with you. Good for lunch breaks on the run. It tastes great and is very filling.

### Ingredients

- 1 Cup (150gm) Mixed Dried Fruit
- 1/3 Cup (75ml) Fresh Orange Juice
- 5 Drops Vanilla Essence
- 4 Tablespoons Butter or Margarine
- 3 Cups (250gm) Quinoa Flakes
- 1/2 Cup Chopped Walnuts
- 1/2 Cup Brown Sugar
- 1 Teaspoon Cinnamon Powder
- 1/2 Teaspoon Salt
- 2 Eggs

### Method

1. To make this Quinoa fruit and nut bar you make a dry mix and a liquid mix and then combine the

2. Put the dried fruit in the orange juice with the vanilla essence.

3. Place to one side to allow the fruit to absorb the liquid.

4. Melt the butter gently and then add the Quinoa flakes and walnuts

5. Cook on a slow heat and turn continuously for 3/4 minutes.

6. Put the flakes mix into a mixing bowl and add the sugar, salt and cinnamon.

7. Return to the fruit mix and add the 2 eggs. mix well.

8. put the 2 mixes together in the mixing bowl and combine well.

9. Press the mixture into a greased square baking tin and bake for 15 minutes in a medium oven.

10. Cut the half cooked mixture into bars and return to the oven for a further 15/20 minutes.

11. Leave to cool for 5 minutes before cutting the bars again and cooling on a baking tray.

# Quinoa Flakes Recipe Ideas

## Simple Porridge

### Ingredients

- 1 Cup Quinoa flakes
- 1 Cup Milk (or water)
- Pinch of Salt

### Method

1. Put all ingredients into a saucepan and slowly bring to the boil.
2. Simmer for 2 or 3 minutes until the mixture thickens.
3. Serve with fresh fruit on top.

## Cheesy Cookies

### Ingredients

- 1/2 Cup Margarine or Butter
- 2 Tbsp Cream Cheese
- 1 1/2 Cups Grated Cheese. Cheddar, Leicester or Gloucester.
- 1 Cup White Flour
- 1/2 Cup Quinoa Flakes
- 1 Tsp Baking Powder
- Large Pinch of Salt
- Pinch of Turmeric - to taste (optional)
- Milk - if needed

### Method

1. Cream the margarine, cream cheese and grated cheese together.
2. In a separate bowl mix the remaining ingredients
3. Combine the 2 mixes into 1 dough - add a little milk if necessary
4. Roll out the dough to about 1/2 inch (12mm) thickness.
5. Cut out with cookie cutter and place on a greased baking tray
6. Bake in a medium oven for about 10 minutes until they start to turn light brown.
7. Cool on a rack and serve

**Black Treacle Flapjack**

**Ingredients**

- 2 Cups Quinoa Flakes
- 1/2 Cup Margarine or Butter
- 2 Tbsp Black Treacle (you can use golden syrup if preferred)
- 1 Cup Plain Flour (you can use Quinoa Flour but it makes a heavier mix)
- 1 Tsp Baking Powder
- Pinch Salt

**Method**

1. Melt the margarine in a sauce pan
2. Add the black treacle and salt.
3. Finally add the flour, baking powder and Quinoa flakes
4. Put in a tray and bake in a medium oven for 20 - 25minutes.
5. The mixture will rise slightly and need to be firm to touch when it is ready.
6. Cut into slices while still hot and allow to cool for 10 minutes before setting out on a cooling tray to finish cooling.
7. Store in an airtight container.

# Section Three - 7 Day Quinoa Diet

This 7 Day Quinoa Diet Plan is a very simple eating plan. It is based on the superfood Quinoa alongside fresh fruit, fresh vegetables and home made juices.

At the end off the week you will have lost 2 – 5 lbs.

You will notice that there are no ridiculous claims here for huge weight loss. You wouldn't believe them anyway and I will not lie to you. The 7 Day Quinoa Diet Plan is about healthy eating as well as moderate weight loss.

The main reason for going on the 7 Day Quinoa Diet Plan is that you will feel healthier and your digestive system will work <u>FOR</u> you and not against you.

The plan is quite simple to follow as I have included a daily meal plan for the complete 7 days. You also have the list of juice recipes and the Quinoa cookbook to help you.

**Here is what the 7 day plan includes.**

- Daily Meal Plan
- Juice Recipes
- Quinoa Recipes
- Snack Food List
- Drinks Allowed
- Quinoa Articles – Taken from My Quinoa Blog www.quinoatips.com and other articles I have had published elsewhere. These articles are packed with background information on Quinoa and why it is so healthy for you.

## FAQ's

### When should I start the diet?

Tomorrow. Today you need to clear out your kitchen of rubbish foods. Then go shopping for the foods you will eat for the next seven days. Use the included shopping list if it helps.

### Can I do the 7 Day Quinoa Diet Plan for longer than one week?

You would need to consult your doctor or a nutritionist on this. I basically follow this diet and will continue to do so from now on as it works for me. I supplement it with some meat protein but not much else.

### Can I drink wine on this diet?

I allow myself the odd glass of red wine but if you want to lose weight on this diet then give it a miss for the seven days. Wine is wasted calories and will stop you losing weight. As I am maintaining my weight loss I can indulge myself once in a while.

### Why Can't I eat Bread?

Bread and other processed carbohydrates is the big, big change in my diet. I used to live on it. These foods really offer no nutritional value to you. I only eat a few slices of bread a week and no white rice, biscuits or cakes.

### Can I substitute any of the Juices?

You can have the same one all week if you choose. I like a bit of variety. You can also swap the meals around to suit yourself.

# The 7 Day Quinoa Diet Plan – Daily Meal Plan

## Day One

### Breakfast

Clear through the gate juice

Ingredients

½ Cucumber

1 Stick Celery

2 Carrots

2 Chopped Basil Leaves (optional)

Method

Do not peel anything. Cut up the cucumber, celery and carrots and juice them with your juicer.

Pour into a large glass with ice and sprinkle the chopped basil leaves over the top

You can also have one item of fresh fruit

### Lunch

Boiled Egg with Green salad. One Item of fresh fruit

### Dinner

Cajun Stir Fry – Serves 2 large portions

Ingredients

- 1/2 cup (100gm) cooked and prepared Quinoa
- 2 Tbsp Olive Oil
- 1 Courgette - sliced
- 6 Mushrooms - sliced
- 1 Onion - chopped
- 1 Red Pepper
- 1 Tin Sweet Corn
- 1 Tsp Cajun Spice Mix (Or more to your taste)
- Salt and Pepper
- 5 Drops Tabasco Sauce

Method

1. Heat the oil in a large pan or wok
2. Fry the vegetables briskly for 5 minutes.
3. Add the spices and Tabasco sauce
4. Serve as it is or in tortilla wraps

## Day Two

## Breakfast

Ginger, spinach and pineapple Juice

Ingredients

Large slice of fresh pineapple

1 Apple

1 Carrot

Handful of Fresh Spinach Leaves

Fresh Root Ginger – amount to taste

Method

Cut the peel off the slice of pineapple. Do not peel the apple or the carrot.

Juice all the ingredients and serve with ice.

You can also have one item of fresh fruit

## Lunch

Fresh vegetables dip. Cut up your favourite vegetables and use a very low fat dip

Plus one item of fresh fruit

## Dinner

Chicken and Quinoa Nutty Stir Fry – Serves 2

Ingredients

· 1/2 Cup (100gm) Cooked and Prepared Quinoa -

This time cooked for only 7/8 minutes so it is a bit crunchier.

- 200 gm Chicken Breast - sliced
- 1/4 Cup (50gm) Pine Nuts
- 1/4 Cup (50gm) Sunflower Seeds
- 1/4 Cup (50gm) Cashew Nuts - chopped
- 1 Carrot - cubed
- 1 Tbsp Sesame Seeds
- 1 Tbsp Olive Oil

Method

1. Cooked the chicken in a large pan or wok with the olive oil.

2. Add the prepared Quinoa and carrots for a further 3 minutes

3. Throw in the remaining ingredients and continue to cook fast for 2 minutes.

4. Serve.

## Day Three

### Breakfast

**Sharp customer Juice**

Ingredients

2 Apples

1 Fresh Beetroot

½ Lime

A Small Handful of Spinach

2 Radishes

Method

Do not peel anything. Simply juice all the ingredients and serve with ice

Plus one item of fresh fruit

### Lunch

Cold meat (100gm) with Green Salad. One Item of fresh fruit

### Dinner

Mixed Beans with Quinoa

Ingredients

- 1/2 Cup (100gm) Cooked and Prepared Quinoa
- 1 Can of Mixed Haricot and Kidney Beans. (I actually use dried beans and do the whole soak and

boil routine but then I am a bit of a food fanatic.)

- 1 Green Pepper Chopped
- 5 Basil Leaves Chopped
- 1 Medium Chilli
- 1 Tin Chopped Tomatoes
- Fresh Salad Leaves

Method

1. Place the Quinoa, beans, chilli, and green pepper in a saucepan

2. Bring to the boil and add the fresh basil leaves

3. Simmer for 10 minutes to allow the flavours to combine

4. Serve on the fresh salad leaves

## Day Four

### Breakfast

#### Tanga Surprise Juice

Ingredients

1 Apple

2 Carrots

Slice of Melon

1 Lime

Piece of Root Ginger – amount to your taste

Method

Do not peel the apple, carrots or the lime; Take the skin off the slice of melon.

Juice all the ingredients and serve.

Plus one item of fruit

### Lunch

#### Quinoa & Tomato Soup

Ingredients

- 1/2 Cup (100gm) of Quinoa
- 8 Ripe Medium Tomatoes (They must be ripe for the best flavour)
- 1 Onion
- 1 Clove Garlic - chopped
- 1 Tsp Oregano or Parsley
- 1/2 Tsp Mixed Herbs

- 4 Cups (½ litre) Water

Method

1. Place the tomatoes, onion, mixed herbs and garlic into a saucepan with the water.

2. Bring to boil and simmer for 5 minutes

3. Add the Quinoa and bring back to the boil

4. Simmer for 15-20 minutes

5. Blend the mixture in a food processor and serve with garnish of oregano

Plus one item of fresh fruit

## Dinner

### Leaf & Warm Mushroom Salad

Ingredients

- 1/2 Cup (100gm) Cooked and Prepared Quinoa
- Handful Cress Leaf
- Handful Baby Spinach
- Handful Rocket Salad
- 3 Spring Onions - chopped
- 6 Mushrooms - sliced
- 1 Tbsp Olive Oil
- 4 Tbsp French Dressing (Or dressing of your choice)

Method

1. Fry the mushrooms in the olive oil until soft and tender.

2. Toss the mushrooms with the other ingredients

3. Drizzle with French dressing and serve immediately

## Day Five

### Breakfast

**Sharp customer Juice**

Ingredients

2 Apples

1 Fresh Beetroot

½ Lime

A Small Handful of Spinach

2 Radishes

Method

Do not peel anything. Simply juice all the ingredients and serve with ice

Plus one item of fresh fruit

### Lunch

Cold meat (100gm) with Green Salad. One Item of fresh fruit

### Dinner

**Quinoa Tomato Sauce with Baked Potato (Sauce is enough for 2 people)**

Ingredients

- Good sized Potatoes for baking in the oven or microwave oven.
- 1/2 Cup (100gm) Quinoa
- 1 Tin of Chopped Tomatoes (or 6 very ripe fresh tomatoes)

- 1 Clove Garlic - chopped
- 4 Medium Mushrooms - sliced
- 1 Onion - chopped
- 4 Tbsp Olive Oil
- 1 Tbsp Chopped Parsley
- 2 Cups (250ml) Vegetable Stock (or Water)
- salt and pepper to taste

Method

1. Bake the potatoes in the oven as normal usually about an hour.

2. To make the sauce first flash fry the garlic, onion and mushrooms until the onion goes clear

3. Add all the remaining ingredients cover and slowly simmer for 20 minutes, turning regularly. The sauce will thicken with the quinoa.

4. Cut the baked potato in half and top with the Quinoa tomato sauce

## Day Six

## Breakfast

### The Coolest Juice

Ingredients

3 Carrots

1 Stick Celery

½ Cucumber

Some Fresh Mint Leaves - chopped

Method

Do not peel anything

Juice the carrots, celery and cucumber, Add the chopped mint and some ice. Stir well and let stand for 2 minutes before drinking.

## Lunch

Boiled egg with Green Salad. One Item of fresh fruit

## Dinner

### Quinoa Ratatouille – Serves 2

Ingredients

- 1/2 Cup (100gm) Cooked and Prepared Quinoa
- 2 Tbsp Olive Oil

- 1 Red Pepper - chopped
- 1 Green Pepper - chopped
- 1 Onion - chopped
- 2 Stick Celery - chopped
- 1 Medium Courgette
- 1 Tbsp Tomato Puree
- 1 Can Chopped Tomatoes
- 4 Drops Tabasco Sauce (optional)
- 1 Tsp Fresh Basil

Method

1. Fry the peppers, onion, celery and courgette for 5 minutes in the olive oil.

2. Add the flavourings and the puree.

3. Finally combine with the chopped tomatoes and Quinoa and bring to the boil

4. Simmer gently for 5 minutes and serve on salad leaves

## Day Seven

### Breakfast

#### Blended Heaven Smoothie

This is made in an electric blender. Not a juicer.

Ingredients

Fresh Strawberries
1 Ripe Banana
4 Ice Cubes
100 ml of Ice Cold Water

Peel and slice the banana
Put all the ingredients into a blender and blend until smooth.

### Lunch

#### Quinoa & Spinach Omelette – serves 2
Ingredients
- 1/2 Cup (100gm) Cooked and Prepared Quinoa
- Olive Oil
- 2 Tablespoons Skimmed Milk
- Handful of Fresh Spinach – chopped
- 1 Red Pepper - chopped
- 4 Eggs
Method

1. Whisk the eggs with the skimmed milk.

2. Blend in the red pepper, Quinoa and spinach

3. Heat up the olive oil in a large frying pan

4. Turn down to a very low heat and cook the omelette slowly in the normal way.

5. Serve with fresh salad

Plus one item of fresh fruit

## Dinner

### Simple Quinoa Salad

Ingredients

- 1/2 Cup (100gm) of Quinoa Grain Cooked and Prepared

- 1 Stick of Celery

- 1 Carrot

- 3 Medium Spring Onions

- 1 Green Pepper

- Salad Leaves

- Italian Balsamic Syrup (Or your preferred Dressing)

Method

1. Chop the celery, spring onions and pepper.

2. Slice the carrot thinly (I use a potato peeler to give me carrot shavings)

3. Toss the ingredients together with the prepared quinoa.

4. Place on a bed of salad leaves and drizzle with the Italian Balsamic Syrup

Can be eaten with cold meat, boiled eggs or fish – 100gm serving for the meat and fish

Well done for completing the 7 day Quinoa diet plan!

# Juice recipes – all recipes serve one person

I always put ice into the glass to cool the juice slightly

The best juices have vegetables in them. They can take some getting used to but they will give you a great start to the day.

The first 6 juices are the ones I use all the time. I have added a few fruit juice recipes at the end of this section for people who can't get used to drinking vegetables.

### Clear through the gate juice – you work it out!

Ingredients

½ Cucumber

1 Stick Celery

2 Carrots

2 Chopped Basil Leaves (optional)

Method

Do not peel anything. Cut up the cucumber, celery and carrots and juice them with your juicer.

Pour into a large glass with ice and sprinkle the chopped basil leaves over the top

# Tanga surprise

Ingredients

1 Apple

2 Carrots

Slice of Melon

1 Lime

Piece of Root Ginger – amount to your taste

Method

Do not peel the apple, carrots or the lime, Take the skin off the slice of melon.

Juice all the ingredients and serve.

# The Coolest

Ingredients

3 Carrots

1 Stick Celery

½ Cucumber

Some Fresh Mint Leaves - chopped

Method

Do not peel anything

Juice the carrots, celery and cucumber, Add the chopped mint and some ice. Stir well and let stand for 2 minutes before drinking.

## Ginger, spinach and pineapple

Ingredients

Large Slice of Fresh Pineapple

1 Apple

1 Carrot

Handful of Fresh Spinach Leaves

Fresh Root Ginger – amount to taste

Method

Cut the peel off the slice of pineapple. Do not peel the apple or the carrot.

Juice all the ingredients and serve with ice

## Sharp customer

Ingredients

2 Apples

1 Fresh Beetroot

½ Lime

A Small Handful of Spinach

2 Radishes

Method

Do not peel anything. Simply juice all the ingredients and serve with ice

# A Late Surprise Entry

Ingredients

2 Carrots

1 Apple

1 Small Parsnip

Some Mint Leaves

Fresh Root Ginger -  small piece

A Few Spinach Leaves

½ Lime

Method

Do not peel anything. Juice everything and  serve with ice

Fruit Juices

## Bitter Sweet

Ingredients

½ Grapefruit

1 Orange

1 Apple

Slice of Fresh Pineapple

Method

Cut the outer skin off the pineapple. Peel the grapefruit and the orange. Do not peel the apple.

Juice all the ingredients and serve with ice

## A Simple Starter

Ingredients

½ Water Melon

½ Cucumber

Sprinkle of Cinnamon (optional)

Method

Peel water melon. Do not peel cucumber. Juice the ingredients and stir in the cinnamon. Serve with ice

## Blended Heaven

This is made in an electric blender. Not a juicer.

Ingredients

Fresh Strawberries

1 Ripe Banana

4 Ice Cubes

100 ml of Ice Cold Water

Peel and slice the banana

Put all the ingredients into a blender and blend until smooth.

# Red Peachy

This is made in an electric blender. Not a juicer.

Ingredients

3 Fresh Peaches

A Few Raspberries

4 Ice Cubes

100 ml of Ice Cold Water

1 Fresh Mint Leaf - chopped (Optional)

Method

Remove the stones from the peaches and chop.

Put all the ingredients into the blender and blend until smooth.

# Snack Food List

Snack food list – All eaten raw except where stated. You do not have to snack on this diet but if you must then this is what to have ready in the kitchen for you to munch on. If you do not have a ready supply of these good foods then you will start snacking on the bad foods.

I have gone even further than this and do not have any banned foods in the house. I only have the healthy food options available to me. When I am out on the road working I am very careful to take some fruit with me as these are the easiest portable snack items I know.

Here is the snack food list:-

Apples

Pear

Orange

Mandarins

Melon

Mango

Pineapple

Grapes – Not too many

Strawberries – No Cream

Banana – Maximum 1 per day

Chick Peas – Boiled and kept in an airtight container in the fridge

Haricot Beans - Boiled and kept in an airtight container in the fridge

Kidney Beans - Boiled and kept in an airtight container in the fridge

Freshly Shucked peas

Celery

Carrot

Broccoli

Cauliflower

Salad Leaves

Sweet Pepper

Tomato

## **Drinks Allowed**

Water – Drink at least 2 litres per day

Black Tea – No Milk

Black Coffee

Herbal Teas such as Earl Grey, Nettle, Green

Fruit teas

Diet canned drinks – 2 per day Maximum

# Quinoa Articles and Background Information

Taken from My Quinoa website www.quinoatips.com and other articles I have published elsewhere. Gives you background information on Quinoa and why it is so healthy for you

### Article 1 - How to Cook Quinoa - Four Different Methods For Preparing Quinoa

### Background information

Quinoa is often thought of as a grain but in fact seeds from a plant. These seeds are small and come in a range of varieties. The most common variety is white which has now become readily available in the UK being stocked by Tesco, Sainsbury's and numerous health food shops. Red Quinoa has recently become available in the UK although I understand that it has been on sale in the U.S. for quite some time.

### The truth about rinsing

For most types you do not need to rinse it. This is because the large manufacturers realized that they would sell more if it was prewashed before going on sale. So I have not found Quinoa on sale that has not been rinsed in the last few months. If it tastes bitter then you need to rinse it by running it under a cold tap for 2 - 3 minutes before cooking.

### What does it taste like?

This superfood has a unique flavour to it. It is compared to rice but it has a definite crunch to it. If you overcook it, it will become soft and fluffy like rice but it will not become sticky and stodgy like overcooked rice does. The flavour is unique but is similar to other grains which is probably why it gets confused with other grains. The best description I can think of is like a mildly crunchy porridge.

### How do you cook it?

The simplest method is to boil it. You take one part of quinoa to two parts of cold water. Bring it to the boil and simmer for 10 - 20 minutes. There are 2 factors that effect the cooking time.

You can slightly under cook the grains for 8 - 10 minutes which gives a much nuttier and crunchy feel. This is the way I prefer it. When it is subsequently added to other ingredients for a bit more cooking it is better to undercook it. In fact one method of cooking (shown below) includes no pre-cooking at all.

## How to microwave these grains

It can be cooked in a microwave quite simply. Using the same ratio of 1 part Quinoa and 2 parts water place them in a microwave dish and cook for 3 minutes. Then leave to stand. Stir for a moment and cook for a further 3 - 5 minutes. Allow to stand for 2 minutes. Any remaining liquid can be drained - it is important that the grains in a microwave are not allowed to go dry.

## Cooking soups and casseroles

This method simply includes Quinoa in soup recipes and casseroles. There is no need to pre-cook the grains in the ways shown above. In soups it can add substance and flavour just by adding it to a favourite recipe. It really is a matter of trying out different soup recipes to find out what you like. Casseroles are very similar.

## How to sprout

Quinoa sprouts are the least impressive sprouts you will ever see. It takes only 2 - 3 days to sprout and must be eaten straight away as it does not keep well. The sprouts are tiny. The benefit of preparing the grains this way is that you can eat it raw. A huge boost for those on a restrictive diet demanding raw food. The protein content is almost legendary and raw it really packs a punch as it is full of nutrients and vitamins. It is best combined with other salad vegetables as it can be quite bland on its own.

## Article 2 - Health Benefits of Quinoa

The ancient seed of Quinoa is so versatile and such an important source of nutrients that it has been referred to as the "gold" of the Incas. It is known to increase stamina, a useful aid in days gone by when "warriors" needed every bit of advantage they could get when their "people" were under attack.

However, such is the structure of Quinoa, it has the benefit of being a natural and complete protein. This means that it has all the amino acids like acid lysine which is very important for the repair and growth of body tissue. As shown below, it is known to be beneficial to the body in a number of ways - nature's natural remedy.

### Migraines and hypertension

Riboflavin and magnesium are the natural aids in Quinoa for bad headaches. They are known to help relax the blood vessels, which reduces constriction and so eases tension. Basically they help the body to function better which in turn eases the stress the body experiences when circumstances make it over work. While no one claims it makes headaches go away, it can help and is known to reduce the frequency of migraine attacks.

### Childhood Asthma

Many allergies are connected with grass seeds but Quinoa is not a grass. It is a plant but is not known to produce serious allergic reactions in people. Asthma is the result of breathing difficulties that are made worse by tension. It is known to have triggers and often there is a family history of asthma. It is known to have got worse over the years and many experts point to our modern living conditions as making it more prevalent. While not all asthma attacks are caused by allergies which may or may not be avoidable, it is known that Quinoa helps to reduce body stress and helps to keep the airways open. It is recommended that children with asthma eat a whole food diet. Many of the nutrients that we need are in Quinoa such as Magnesium which naturally helps to reduce spasms in the bronchial tubes. We know that many asthma sufferers are short of vitamin b, minerals like magnesium, zinc and iron all of which can be found in Quinoa. Why not check out some of the recipes and see which ones are easiest to include in your child's diet.

### Gallstones

This is another surprising area where Quinoa is known to be useful. It may not get rid of gallstones but it can help protect their development. Indeed this is another case where a wholesome diet rich in fiber can aid in the digestion of foodstuffs. As it is a soluble fiber it speeds through the intestines and reduces the need of increased bile production. Too much bile production helps to develop gallstones so this is another natural remedy for our bodies.

## Type 2 Diabetes

Quinoa is rich in magnesium which is a mineral that is essential in the body's ability to deal with glucose and insulin. Yet again there is evidence that Quinoa, as part of a whole food diets aids in the digestion of foods. It is also known to increase Insulin sensitivity while reducing triglycerides (blood fats which need to be kept low in diabetics).

## Heart Disease

Quinoa is known to prevent the clogging of arteries and veins which in turn helps to relieve stresses on the heart. The fat in Quinoa is good fat in that is low in cholesterol and can help reduce blood pressure thanks to the presence of potassium and magnesium. In other words it is a good source of protein without the drawbacks of too much saturated fat and cholesterol.

## Pregnant Mums

Quinoa is known to be an endurance food which gives energy. It is also known to be a good source of Iron which pregnant mums are always advised to increase in their diet. It is good for tissue repair and development of teeth and bones. Along with the other benefits of Quinoa, it is a useful source of goodness that forming babies will demand in plenty as they grow. It is also good for Mums when they are feeding as it will improve the quality of milk for new-born infants.

## Cataracts

Quinoa is thought to help prevent cataracts and may aid those with the condition. Studies have shown that people who absorb about 99 grams of protein were only half as likely to develop nuclear cataracts(light is difficult to pass through the centre of the eye) while those with the greater polyunsaturated fats about 17 grams a day were 30 percent likely not to develop problems with the outer lens(corticular cataracts).

Nowadays, we are looking more and more to natural foods. We all know the benefits of fibre in our diet but until more recently we have forgotten about Quinoa.

## Article 3 - Is Quinoa Gluten Free?

Quinoa is a fantastic food full of nutrients and vitamins. Quinoa is a vegetable protein that the body finds easy to break down and digest. It also has a far lower fat content than most meat.

For people who need to follow a gluten free diet regime the good news is that standard quinoa grains are gluten free. Quinoa grain can be included into your diet easily and you can be sure that as long as the other ingredients are also gluten free there will be no problem.

There are however Quinoa food products where it is not quite so clear cut. Quinoa flour and Quinoa flakes are processed Quinoa and cannot be guaranteed gluten free. The problem comes because some Quinoa manufacturers use the same factory to produce other flours. This means that there can be some cross contamination with wheat flour products.

Obviously if your gluten problem is not too severe then you could probably cope with this slight risk. (No promises here - check with your doctor)

You hear of people reacting to nuts so violently that it can be a concern but Quinoa doesn't have the same level of reaction that nuts do.

If you are merely gluten intolerant rather than allergic to gluten this will not be a problem for you. Using Quinoa flakes in particular is a very flexible way of eating Quinoa. More recipes and cooking methods are coming out all the time.

Quinoa Flour is much harder to use in normal baking without adding ordinary flour. There are quinoa bread makers but this is like rye bread and is quite heavy. But if you like rye bread you will enjoy Quinoa bread. In the UK both Tesco and Sainbury's occasionally have stock of Quinoa bread.

The good news however is that the standard form of Quinoa as "grains" is gluten free. It is also very high in essentials proteins and vitamins. Quinoa is good for you!

More and more suppliers of Quinoa are pre-washing the Quinoa which means that most or all of the bitter saponin coating has been rinsed off before being packed.

As well as the health benefits of Quinoa, we have found it to be easy to cook and very enjoyable to eat.

## Article 4 - What Is Quinoa And Why Can It Help Your Body Heal?

Quinoa is pronounced "keen-wah". It is a South American plant , an ancient super food that has been rediscovered in recent years. It is a fantastic source of protein and slow releasing carbohydrates suitable for meat lovers and vegetarians alike.

It is a versatile food that can be used in salads, stir fries, soups, stews, casseroles and even desserts.

Quinoa originated in South America and was used by the ancient Incas. It was regarded as a sacred food and valued for its amazing properties. The quinoa we buy is the seed of this plant and is sometimes called the mother grain.

Quinoa is a lot like millet to look at but is flattened with a pointed oval shape. Although not a true cereal grain, it can be treated as a grain in cooking and is usually cooked like rice. It can also be sprouted.

Quinoa is classed as a vegetable protein which is easy to digest. It is brilliant when used as an ingredient in weight loss diets as its slow releasing carbohydrates help to maintain blood sugar levels. This is a also a great benefit for people who are diabetic. Quinoa is known to be beneficial to both kidney and bladder complaints as it contains all the essential amino acids.

It is a complete protein but much easier to digest than most meat proteins. This makes it an ideal addition to both vegan and vegetarian diets. It offers more iron than other grains and contains high levels of potassium and riboflavin, to say nothing of B vitamins, B6, niacin and thiamin. It is also a good source of zinc, copper and manganese.

Perhaps the best feature is that it is gluten free. People with asthma and allergies usually find that it is non allergenic which is helpful because Quinoa is quite filling and substantial. As you cook Quinoa the external germ forms a band around each grain and spirals out forming a tail. It is this tail that gives it its own unique texture which seems to complement the delicate flavour of the seed part.

It is often used as a meat substitute in vegetarian dishes and can even be eaten raw when sprouted for salads. Is is also wonderful as a thickener in soups.

## Article 5 - Ways To Sprout Quinoa Grains

As a quinoa enthusiast and author I have come to the conclusion that I knew all there was to know about preparing it.

I was proved wrong over the weekend by what happened most unexpectedly in my fridge at home. I have taken recently to eating Quinoa raw by soaking it for 8 hours and including it in salads and stir fry dishes. This weekend I had far too much prepared for my meal so I put the remainder in the fridge. It stayed there overnight.

The following day I thought I would use the grains up in a stir fry dish for dinner. When I took the Quinoa out of the fridge it had sprouted perfectly. In fact the sprouts were better and bigger than the ones I had previously done in a proper sprouting unit I have.

I have now abandoned the method I have been using for 2 years in favour of the following method for sprouting Quinoa.

### Sprouting Quinoa Grains - Method 2

1.  Rinse the required amount of Quinoa in a sieve.

2.  Immerse in water for 8 hours

3.  Rinse once more

4.  Place the soaked Quinoa in a bowl in the fridge for about 12 hours

The grains will have sprouted with long thin tails. The grains can be combined with salad ingredients just as other types of sprouts. They can also be thrown into a stir fry dish with courgettes, mushrooms and other vegetables of your choice.
The tails are bigger and longer than those I have had in my sprouting unit and they seem to taste better. To top it all this is half the time it use to take using the other method.

I have had very consistent results with white/cream grains so far. I am now going to experiment with red Quinoa although I am pretty sure they will work just as well. Yet again I am surprised at the versatility of this fantastic grain.

## Article 6 - Will Quinoa Ever Replace Wheat in Our Diet?

Most of us eat wheat in bread and breakfast cereals on a daily basis. Most of us eat far too much highly processed wheat in the form of white bread and processed ready meals. In the last 20 years there has been a swing to eating whole wheat grains and that has become acknowledged as the healthier option. We do however eat too much processed wheat and this has led to an increase of food intolerances and allergies. In fact wheat has now become very allergenic due to its excessive consumption in the developed world.

### People are looking for alternative grains

There has been an increasing demand for alternative due to illnesses and conditions such as celiac disease. People with celiac disease cannot intake gluten. There are a wide range of symptoms which are beyond the range of this article.

Because of this there has been move to eat a wider range of grains in our diet. Many of these are far more nutritious than wheat and do not have the associated health problems. Quinoa, although not truly a grain has been at the forefront of this move and is now gaining wide acceptance as a healthy and nutritious alternative. Quinoa is gluten free and highly nutritious. It comes in grain form as well as flour and flakes.

### How useable is Quinoa in food preparation

Of course you cannot make white bread out of Quinoa. The Quinoa flour is not like wheat flour and is much heavier. You can make cookies and tray bakes with it but you will never bake a standard loaf of bread with it.

The minds of consumers need to look again at their staple foods and reconsider if bread, pizzas, muffins and other wheat rich food products are really necessary as part of a 21st century diet. Sure they are quick and easy to prepare but at what cost to our health.

Quinoa is not the mystery grain that it was 10 years ago and is now becoming readily available in our supermarkets. More and more excellent Quinoa recipes are being researched and produced.

### The answer to the question

Quinoa will not ever replace wheat but it will find a place in most people's kitchens over the next 10 years due to its unbeatable vitamin and nutrition profile

## Article 7 - What is the Difference Between Quinoa and Amaranth?

Quinoa grains and amaranth grains look so similar that you wonder if they are in fact the same product.

They do come from the same family of plants and nutritionally they are quite similar but there are differences.

Both of South American origins the Aztecs grew amaranth as a staple food while the Incas grew Quinoa. The growing conditions needed for both are exactly the same. In fact they both grow well in difficult conditions and poor soil. Their indigenous growing location was at high altitude in the mountains. In modern times they are grown in the USA and South America and with improved growing conditions both plants are easy to produce. They crop 3 - 6 months from sowing.

The 2 main differences from a culinary perspective are:-

### Size of the grains

Amaranth seeds are quite a bit smaller than Quinoa grains. They come in the same colours of white, cream, red or black although I have to say I have only ever seen the white and cream available in the shops. You would probably have to grow your own to get the others. They are better for thickening soups and casseroles as they almost disappear in long cooking times. The appearance of both grains is similar and they both have the familiar "tail" after cooking. (try it and see)

### Saponins

Quinoa has a coating of saponins which have a bitter taste. these have to be rinsed off before cooking. Amaranth does not have these saponins and so does not need the same level of preparations. The coating of these saponins has been a problem in getting quinoa onto the dinner plate of the western world. In the last 3 or 4 years manufacturers have been prewashing the Quinoa so that now you usually do not need to pre-wash the Quinoa.

To summarise, Both these grains have almost identical nutritional profiles. The smaller size of the amaranth grain will lend itself to the soups, curries and casseroles type of dishes. The quinoa grain will always be better for salads and stir fry dishes where the Quinoa can still be seen as well as eaten.

## Article 8 - Using Quinoa As a Replacement For Rice and Cous Cous

Quinoa is very versatile in the kitchen. One of the simplest ways of using it is as a straight replacement for rice or cous cous. Now if you are interested in authentic Indian curries or Moroccan cuisine then you are not going to want to substitute anything for the correct ingredients.

But it is actually a very healthy alternative because it is full of vitamins and nutrients. It also has a nutty and crunchy texture that lends itself very well to these dishes.

### Quinoa instead of rice.

This very simple substitution works very well for mild and medium spiced foods. If you like hot curries then Quinoa is not quite as good as rice at reducing the strength of the food. In this case it is best to over cook the Quinoa to help combat the spiciness of the curry.
For other dishes such as tabouleh and risotto it is ideal instead of rice. I would say preferable to rice because you do not get the starchiness. No post rinsing is needed. You can serve it straight from the pan. You can use it instead of rice in desserts but it does not perform as well here as with the savoury dishes.

### Quinoa instead of cous cous

Cous cous is found very often in salads mixed with other vegetables. You can combine it with peppers and green leaf salads to make an endless combination of quickly prepared meals. Quinoa is an ideal replacement for cous cous but it does not keep as well once it has been prepared. You can keep it in a fridge for 2 days in an airtight container quite safely. After that it can lose its texture. It is better to prepare what you need on the day. Any left overs can be used as a packed lunch snack.

The best way of finding out about replacing rice and cous cous with Quinoa is simply to try it. Be adventurous and you will find it very easy to use in your favourite recipes.

## Article 9 - Where Does Quinoa Come From?

The indigenous people of Bolivia have been cultivating "the rice if the Incas" for over 5000 years. Today it is more widely available since financial support has been provided for the growing, harvesting and export of this amazing food. It is very much the golden grain of the Andes and is a superb alternative to rice or pasta

### The supply chain for Quinoa

There are over 200 farms in Bolivia that grow and supply Quinoa to an ever increasing demand. Other countries in South America also now produce Quinoa and the vast majority support organic growing systems and operate under the "Fairtrade" system. This means that the original farmers directly benefit from the increasing trade in Quinoa, not just the large companies.

### The Mother Grain

One of the most sacred foods of the the ancient Incas of South America was Quinoa - a plant so nourishing, delicious and vital they called it "chesiya mama", the mother grain. It is also known as the rice of the Incas.

### Superior Benefits

Quinoa is superior to other grains because it is a complete protein, containing 8 essential amino acids. It is actually a seed, not a grain, and is gluten free. When cooked, the grain itself is soft and delicate, but the germ is crunchy, creating a delicious combination of flavour and texture.
It is an excellent meat substitute in vegetarian dishes. It can be used in stir-fries, soups, stews, salads and many more of your favourite recipes. Quinoa is ready to eat with minimal cooking. It can also be sprouted and then eaten raw. A standard portion size would be 60 - 80g uncooked weight per person.

## Article 10 - Quinoa is Not a True Grain - It is a Seed

Quinoa is known as a grain and for cooking and eating purposes it can be treated as a grain but it is in fact a seed. The plant we get quinoa from is the goosefoot plant - technical name Chenopodium. It is grown mainly in South America and some parts of the USA. It is closely related to spinach and swiss chard. The plant bears the seeds after flowering about 6 months from sowing although modern growing methods are reducing this cropping cycle. With this 6 month cycle farmers can get 2 crop cycles a year but research is currently looking at trying to achieve 3 Quinoa crops per year. This is pretty intensive but reflects the increasing popularity of Quinoa.

You can use the leaves from the goosefoot plant in salads and as a vegetable in other dishes but this has to be fresh due to the fact that it doesn't store well.

### Being a grain makes little difference to how you use it

The fact that quinoa is a seed and not a grain makes little difference from the point of view of cooking. It is usually cataloged with grains and can be substituted for most grains without a problem. The high protein content of Quinoa makes it highly desirable for inclusion in your diet. The only facet of Quinoa that may cause a problem in converting recipes is that it has a slightly higher fat content and some baking dishes such as scones and flapjacks may be slightly more oily than you would like.

### What you do with quinoa

For use as an accompaniment to hot spice and savoury dishes it is ideal. An improvement on white rice with its crunchy texture and slightly nutty taste. The easiest way to use it is in salads mixed with other vegetables such as peppers, celery and sweet corn. Being a seed it can also be sprouted. This takes only a couple of days and the raw Quinoa sprouts are highly nutritious if a little bland. They are best mixed in with other ingredients.

# Article 11 - 3 Reasons Why Quinoa Will Never Make You Fat

Quinoa is becoming recognized in the 21st century as a "super food". Nutritionists are singing the praises of its complete protein profile and the high vitamin count. The farmers who produce the grain in South America are getting organized and increasing the growing production through the excellent fair trade scheme. In the UK I think all the Quinoa available is "fairtrade".

So collectively we are eating more Quinoa which is very good for us. But can you overeat on Quinoa. Could it just be a fad and then we will discover that too much Quinoa is bad for you. Well I think this is very unlikely for the following 3 reasons.

## Reasons 1 - Quinoa is very filling

A standard serving would be 60 - 80 grams uncooked weight. This is plenty and you will find it very satisfying. If you were to double up the portion size I guarantee you would not be able to consume it all. The seeds are a bit like eating porridge in that they take a long time for your system to digest. You are not going to be hungry for a few hours after eating quinoa because of this.

## Reason 2 - Quinoa is eaten with other healthy foods

When you cook and prepare Quinoa it is automatic to use it with other healthy foods. That is the way it works. You would never mix it with sugary sweet foods or fatty meals such as a fry up. Where would you put Quinoa in a fry up?? The foods you mix it with are fresh vegetables and fruit. This makes the best use of its features and benefits.

## Reason 3 - Quinoa is not a fast food

You have to prepare it and put it in recipes to get the best advantage. It does keep for a couple of days in a refrigerator but you would still mix it with other things to eat it. It really is part of a statement about the way you eat and live your life. Eating any grains is going to improve your health and having them as part of your staple diet means that you will not overeat and get fat.

## Article 12 - Quinoa Can Be Good For Sufferers of Irritable Bowel Syndrome – IBS

Irritable bowel syndrome - IBS - is a debilitating stomach disorder that many suffer from. It can completely stop you from living your life normally. The disorder is not ever present for most sufferers. It comes for a time due to perhaps an unknown food intolerance or a mad phase of binge eating. You can also develop the disorder through stress or as a result of other illness. You recover from the illness to find yourself suffering from IBS. There are some people who live with it almost constantly and they have to regularly monitor their diet and medication to achieve some semblance of normal life.

### Quinoa as part of the solution

Quinoa is a good food for inclusion in a diet for people who have IBS. It is very good for many stomach and digestive problems because it is easy to digest but still has a very high fiber content. It also has a very high protein count and is described as a complete protein. The other benefit of Quinoa is that it is one of the least allergenic foods. It is completely natural and unprocessed so doesn't create problems and surprises for people who need to watch their diet carefully.

### How to help by using Quinoa in your diet

Quinoa is not a cure all but as part of a strategy to improve the diet it is ideal. It is also very easy to include into an IBS preventative regime. It is most commonly used as an accompaniment to savory dishes instead of rice and pasta. This substitution on its own will help a lot of people straight away.

You can eat it as a type of porridge for breakfast with fresh fruit. You can also sprout it for use in salads.

Most people who suffer from IBS need to find easy wholesome foods to help solve their health problem and Quinoa certainly will fit in with this aim.

LaVergne, TN USA
02 August 2010
191771LV00007B/206/P